STARTERS ACTIVITIES

Sculpture

Macdonald Educational

About Starters Activities

These books cover a variety of activities for children at school or at home. The projects with their step-by-step illustrations, require the minimum of help from teachers or parents. Most of the words in the text will be in the reading vocabulary of the majority of young readers. Word and sentence length have also been carefully controlled. Extra information and more complex activities are included at the end of each book. Where possible, the child is free to invent and experiment on his own, but concise instructions are given wherever necessary. Teachers and experts have been consulted on the content and accuracy of these books.

Illustrated by: Robin Arkell

Managing Editor: Su Swallow

Editor: Jennifer Vaughan

Production: Stephen Pawley, Rosemary Bishop

Reading consultant: Donald Moyle, author of *The Teaching of Reading* and senior lecturer in education at Edge Hill College of Education

Chairman, teacher advisory panel: F. F. Blackwell, director of the primary extension programme, National Council for Educational Technology

Teacher panel: Stephanie Connell, Sally Chaplin

Colour reproduction by:
Colourcraftsmen Limited

ISBN 0 356 04397 5

Made and printed in Great Britain by:
Adams Bros. and Shardlow Ltd, Leicester

Filmsetting by:
Layton-Sun Limited

First published in 1973 by
Macdonald and Company
(Publishers) Limited
St Giles House
49-50 Poland Street
London W1

Contents

Look at all these things.
What can you make with them?

Carving

Try making models out of soap.
Use a spoon to cut the soap.

Candle wax models
can be made this way too.
Here are some candle wax models.

Twig sculpture

Make a sculpture with twigs.
Use clay and sticky tape.

A balloon man

You need these things
to make a balloon man.
You will also need
the middle of a toilet roll.

Blow up the balloon and tie the end.
Stick it to a toilet roll middle.
Stand the toilet roll middle on a bottle.
Stick toilet paper all over the balloon.

Stick paper over the eggshells
to make eyes.
Now paint the balloon man.
Try making balloon animals.

Cardboard sculpture

Cut some cardboard into pieces.
Cut a slit in each piece.

Fit the pieces together
to build a model.
Put big pieces at the bottom.

Nails and wood

Here is a pattern of nails in wood.

Nail different things to a piece of wood.
Here are some of the things
you might use.

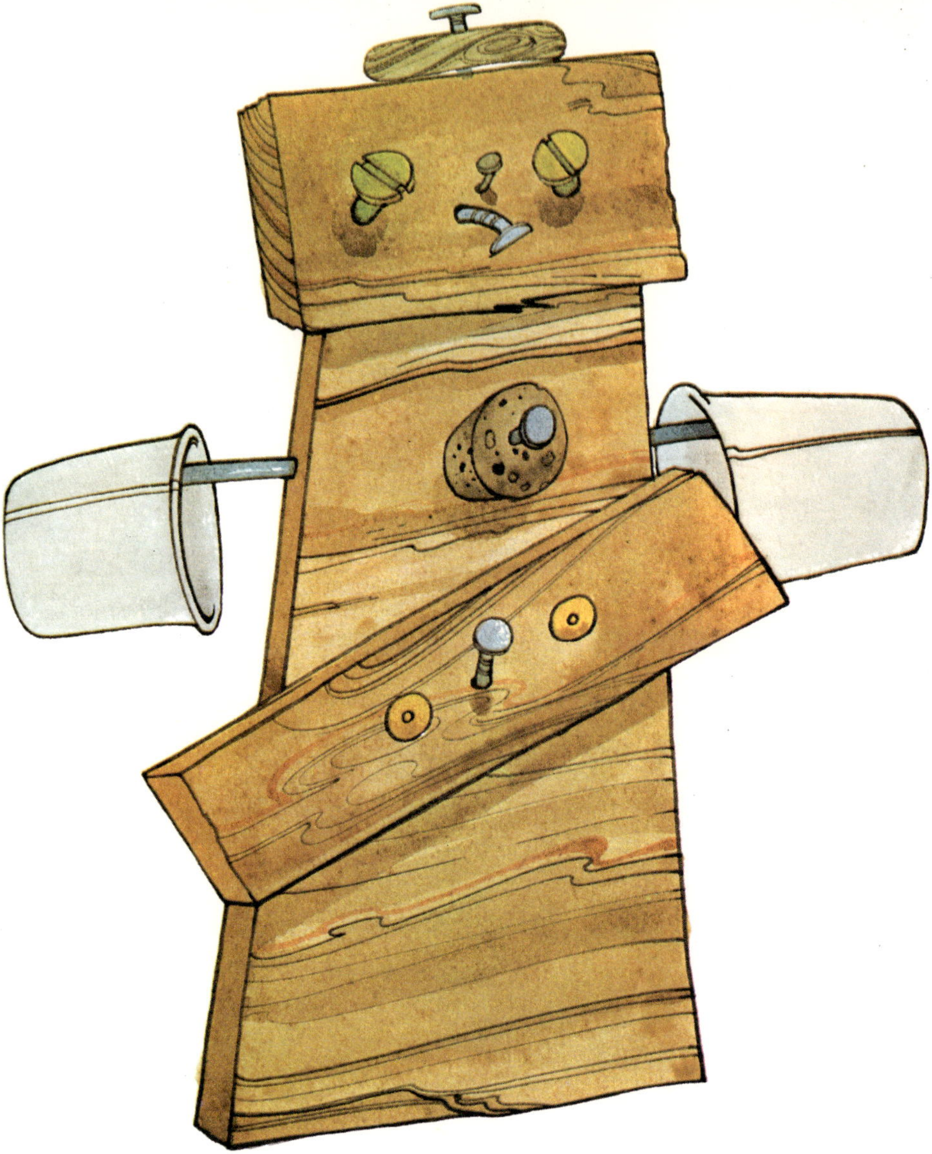

Nail pieces of wood together.
Make a sculpture from them.

Spacemen

Make a big spaceman from egg boxes, toilet roll middles, and cardboard.

Try making a small spaceman.
Use cardboard and yoghourt pots.
Cover him with silver paper.

Vegetable animals

Make this animal from vegetables.

Try making a vegetable zoo.
Use sticks or nails for legs.

A turnip head

Ask someone to cut a turnip in half.
Scoop out each half
with a spoon.

Make a face like this
from the two halves.
You might put a small candle inside.

Wire sculpture

Use wire to make shapes.
Use thin wire and pipe cleaners.

Make shapes with thick wire.
Make coat hanger people.
Try making coat hanger
animals too.

Dress your coat hanger people
in cloth and cardboard.

Sculpture words

soap
(page 2)

sticky tape
(page 4)

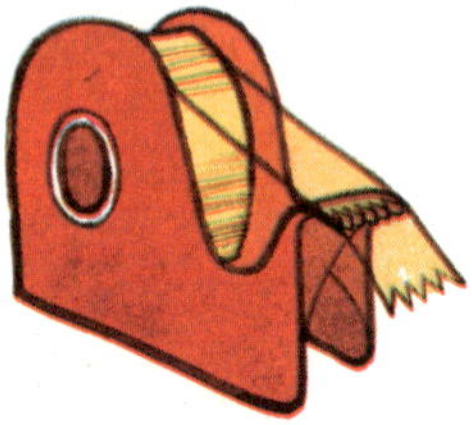

spoon
(page 2)

balloon
(page 5)

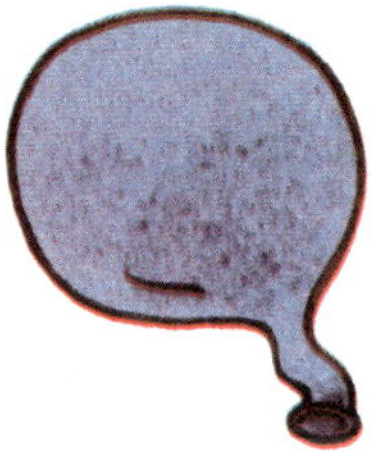

candle
(page 3)

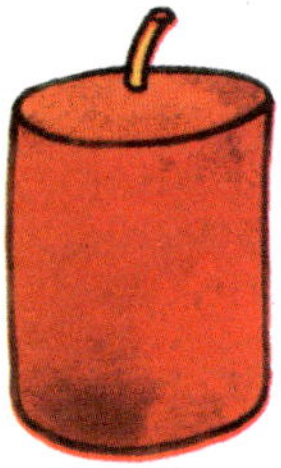

eggshell
(page 5)

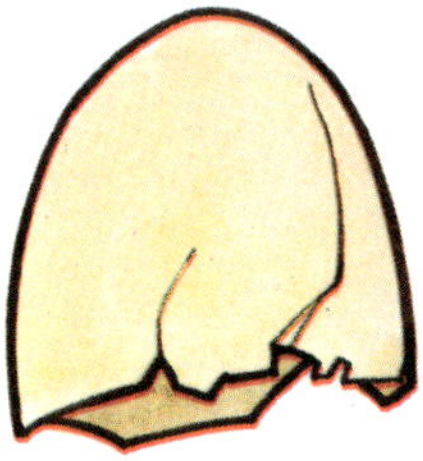

twig
(page 4)

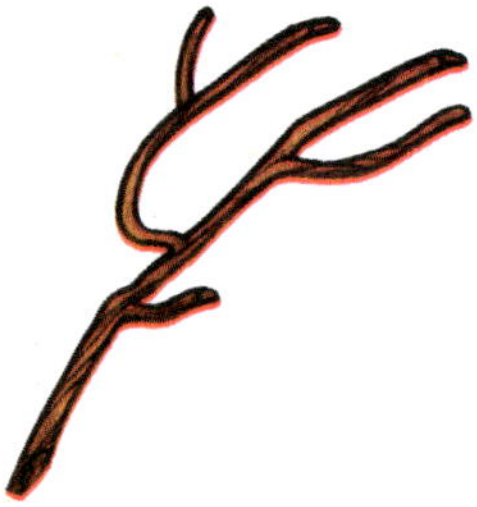

glue
(page 5)

cardboard
(page 8)

slit
(page 8)

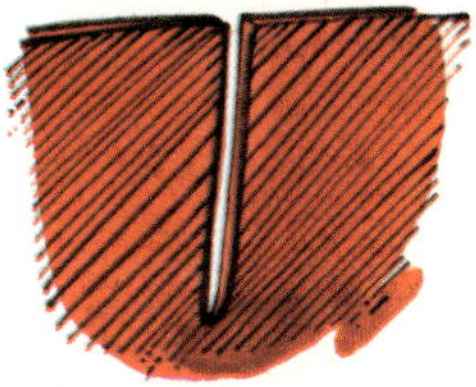

nails
(page 10)

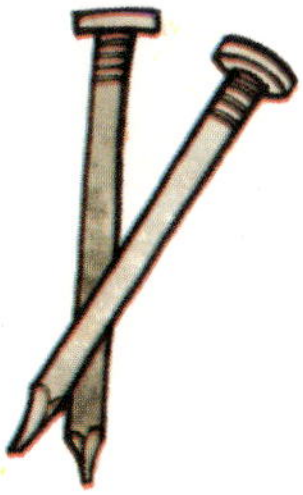

wood
(page 10)

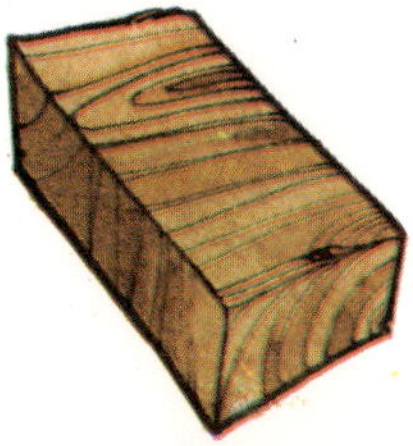

egg box
(page 13)

vegetables
(page 15)

turnip
(page 17)

wire
(page 19)

pipe
cleaner
(page 19)

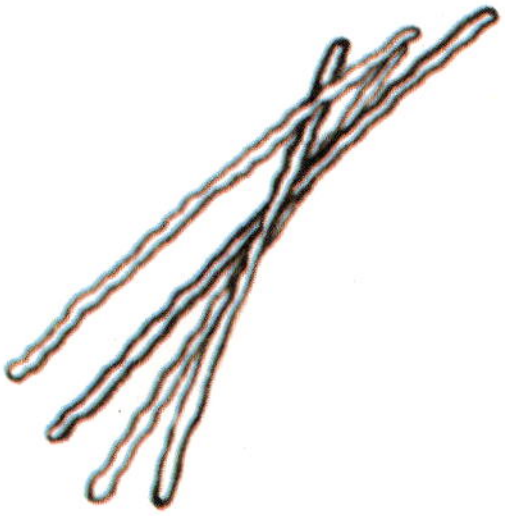

coat
hanger
(page 20)

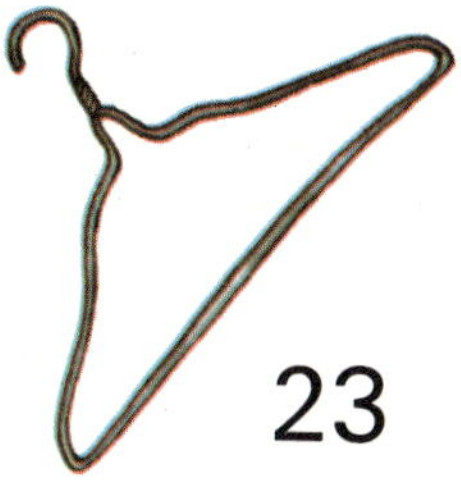

Remember

Wear an apron
if you are painting
or glueing.
Roll up your sleeves.

Tidy up
when you have finished working.
Wipe the table clean.

You might need to use
a sharp knife. If you do,
always ask a grown-up
to help. Do not use
the knife yourself.

Some glue comes
in tubes like this.
Always put the top back
when you have finished
with it.

Some harder projects

Home-made modelling clay

Try making your own modelling clay. You will need two cups of flour, one cup of salt and some water. Mix the flour and salt with enough water to make a stiff dough. If possible, it is a good idea to add a quarter of a cup of powdered alum (which you can buy from an art shop) to the mixture. This will help to keep your clay fresh, though it will work without it. Try using this clay to make model insects. Give them clay bodies and pipe cleaner or match stick legs. Try using kitchen foil for wings. You can paint your model when the clay is dry.

Candle sculpture

On page 3 we tell you how to carve models from candle wax using a sharp teaspoon. These carvings can be made more interesting by painting the candle first. Mix powder paint with washing-up liquid to make a thick paint which will stick to a candle. Paint the candle, and then let the paint dry. Now cut a pattern into the candle with the same kind of sharp teaspoon you used before.

Stone sculpture

Use strong glue (the sort that carpenters use) to stick stones together to make stone models. Use two round stones to make a cat. Try using wool or string to make a tail and some whiskers. You could paint the cat when the glue is dry.

Some harder projects

Turnip tops

Find a small turnip and stick a clay nose, mouth and ears on to it. It is best to have the root end of the turnip at the top of the head, and the part where the leaves were at the bottom. Paste thin strips of newspaper all over the turnip head. Let the paper dry. Now add hair or a beard if you want to, and paint the turnip head. Push a thick knitting needle or a stick up into the head, so that you can use it as a puppet. Try making a whole family of turnip tops.

Balsa wood totem pole

Use a block of balsa wood to make a totem pole. Wrap some sandpaper tightly around a pencil and fasten it with sticky tape. Use this as a file to rub the balsa wood. You can make patterns of crosses and zig-zags on the wood with the file. When you have finished, paint the totem pole in bright colours.